The Burial at Thebes

The Burial at Thebes

Sophocles' *Antigone*

TRANSLATED BY SEAMUS HEANEY

faber and faber

First published in 2004
by Faber and Faber Limited
3 Queen Square, London WC1N 3AU

This paperback edition first published in 2005
Typeset by Country Setting, Kingsdown, Kent CT14 8ES
Printed and bound in Great Britain by T. J. International Ltd, Padstow, Cornwall

A CIP record for this book
is available from the British Library

ISBN 0–571–22362–1

2 4 6 8 10 9 7 5 3 1

for Marianne McDonald

Dramatis Personae

Antigone

Ismene
her sister

Chorus
of Theban elders

Creon
King of Thebes

Guard

Haemon
Creon's son

Tiresias

Messenger

Eurydice
Creon's wife

The scene is Thebes, in front of Creon's palace, just as the dawn is breaking. Antigone and Ismene enter hastily.

Antigone

Ismene, quick, come here!
What's to become of us?
Why are we always the ones?

There's nothing, sister, nothing
Zeus hasn't put us through
Just because we are who we are –
The daughters of Oedipus.
And because we are his daughters
We took what came, Ismene,
In public and in private,
Hurt and humiliation –
But this I cannot take.

No, wait.
　　　　Here's what has happened.
There's a general order issued
And again it hits us hardest.
The ones we love, it says,
Are enemies of the state.
To be considered traitors –

Ismene

How so? What do you mean?

Antigone

I mean – have you not heard?

Ismene

What I heard was enough.
Our two brothers are dead,
The Argos troops withdrawn
And the pair of us left to cope.
But what's next, I don't know.

Antigone

That's why I came outside.
The walls in there have ears.
This is for your ears only.

Ismene

What is it? You have me scared.

Antigone

And right you are to be scared.
Creon has made a law.
Eteocles has been buried
As a soldier, with full honours,
So he's gone home to the dead.
But not Polyneices.
Polyneices is denied
Any burial at all.

Word has come down from Creon.
There's to be no laying to rest,
No mourning, and the corpse
Is to be publicly dishonoured.
His body's to be dumped,
Disposed of like a carcass,
Left out for the birds to feed on.

2

If you so much as throw him
The common handful of clay
You'll have committed a crime.

This is law and order
In the land of good King Creon.
This is his edict for you
And for me, Ismene, for me.
And he's coming to announce it.
'I'll flush 'em out,' he says.
'Whoever isn't for us
Is against us in this case.
Whoever breaks this law,
I'll have them stoned to death.'

                I say,
He has put it to us.
                I say
It's a test you're facing,
Whether you are who you are,
And true to all you belong to,
Or whether –

Ismene

Antigone . . .
              Antigone,
What do you mean, a test?
If things have gone this far
What is there I can do?

Antigone

You can help me do one thing.

Ismene

And what thing is that?

Antigone

His body . . . Help me to lift
And lay your brother's body.

Ismene

And bury him, no matter . . .?

Antigone

Are we sister, sister, brother?
Or traitor, coward, coward?

Ismene

But what about Creon's order?

Antigone

What are Creon's rights
When it comes to me and mine?

Ismene

Easy now, my sister.
Think this through for a minute.
Think of the line we come from:
We're children of Oedipus –
Daughters of the man
Who fathered us on his mother –
The king they drove from their city.
No matter he didn't know.
No matter it was Oedipus
Brought his own crimes to light
And then reached into his eyes
And tore them out of their sockets –
Still they drove him out.
Oedipus had to perish.
And then his wife, the mother
Who bared her breasts for him

4

In the child-bed and the bride-bed,
She hanged herself in a noose.

And now this last thing happens.
The doom in our blood comes back
And brother slaughters brother –
The two of them, dead in a day.

Are you and I to be next?
How do you think they see us?
How do you think we'd fare
If we went against the order?
Two women on our own
Faced with a death decree –
Women, defying Creon?
It's not a woman's place.
We're weak where they are strong.
Whether it's this or worse,
We must do as we're told.

In the land of the living, sister,
The laws of the land obtain –
And the dead know that as well.
The dead will have to forgive me.
I'll be ruled by Creon's word.
Anything else is madness.

Antigone
You and the laws of the land!
Sister, let me tell you:
From now on, and no matter
How your mind may change,
I'll never accept your help.
I will bury him myself.
And if death comes, so be it.

5

There'll be a glory in it.
I'll go down to the underworld
Hand in hand with a brother.
And I'll go with my head held high.
The gods will be proud of me.

The land of the living, sister,
Is neither here nor there.
We enter it and we leave it.
The dead in the land of the dead
Are the ones you'll be with longest.
And how are you going to face them,
Ismene, if you dishonour
Their laws and the gods' law?

Ismene

Dishonour them I do not.
But nor am I strong enough
To defy the laws of the land.

Antigone

Live, then; and live with your choice.
I am going to bury his body.

Ismene

I fear for you, Antigone.

Antigone

Better fear for yourself.

Ismene

Oh stop! This must never get out.

Antigone

No. No. Broadcast it.
Your cover-ups sicken me.

I have nothing to hide
From the powers that see all.
I'm doing what has to be done.

Ismene

What are you, Antigone?
Hot-headed or cold-blooded?
This thing cannot be done.

Antigone

But it still has to be tried.

Ismene

You're mad. You don't have a chance.

Antigone

Here and now, Ismene,
I hate you for this talk.
And the dead are going to hate you.
Call me mad if you like
But leave me alone to do it.
If Creon has me killed,
Where's the disgrace in that?
The disgrace would be to avoid it.

Exit Antigone.

Ismene

Nothing's going to stop you.
But nothing's going to stop
The ones that love you, sister,
From keeping on loving you.

Exit Ismene.

Enter Chorus of Theban elders.

Chorus
> Glory be to brightness, to the gleaming sun,
> Shining guardian of our seven gates.
> Burn away the darkness, dawn on Thebes,
> Dazzle the city you have saved from destruction.
>
> Argos is defeated, the army beaten back,
> > All their brilliant shields
> Smashed into shards and smithereens.
>
> Like a golden eagle, the enemy came swooping,
> Like an eagle screaming down the sky,
> Hoping to set fire to the seven towers.
> But the dragon of Thebes had grown teeth.
> We overwhelmed him on the walls
> And Zeus blasted his overbearing.
>
> A god of war stiffened our will
> And locked our arms, so the line held.
>
> *Glory be to brightness, to the gleaming sun.*
>
> Seven guardians at our seven gates
> Bore the brunt and broke the charge.
> > Our attackers
> Were struck down and stripped of their armour.
> Their spears and helmets are the spoils of war.
> We have hung their shields among the trophies.
>
> But Polyneices and Eteocles:
> The only trophies they took at Thebes
> Were each other's deaths. Their doom was sealed.
> Their banners flew, the battle raged
> And they fell together, their father's sons.
>
> *Glory be to brightness, to the gleaming sun.*

Glory be to Victory. I can feel her wings
                    Fanning the air.
The joy in my eyes is like the joy in hers
Dazzling the city she has saved from destruction.

Race the chariots and run to the temples.
Drum the earth from early until late.
Give glory to the god of the dance.
Let Bacchus lead us and burn away the dark!
Glory be to brightness, to the gleaming world.

Enter Creon with his guards.

King Creon. All hail to Creon.
He's a new king but he's right
For this city at this moment.
Now we will know what's what,
Why he has sent for us
To be privy to his thinking.

Creon

Gentlemen. We have entered calmer waters.
Our ship of state was very nearly wrecked
But the gods have kept her safe.
                              So, friends, well done.
You from the start have been a loyal crew.
You stood by Oedipus when he was at the helm
And when his sons stepped in to take his place
You stood by them as well. But now they're gone,
Two brothers badged red with each other's blood,
And I, as next of kin to those dead and doomed,
I'm next in line. The throne has come to me.

Until a man has passed this test of office
And proved himself in the exercise of power,

He can't be truly known – for what he is, I mean,
In his heart and mind and capabilities.
Worst is the man who has all the good advice
And then, because his nerve fails, fails to act
In accordance with it, as a leader should.
                              And equally to blame
Is anyone who puts the personal
Above the overall thing, puts friend
Or family first. But rest assured:
My nerve's not going to fail, and there's no threat
That's going to stop me acting, ever,
In the interests of all citizens. Nor would I,
Ever, have anything to do
With my country's enemy. For the patriot,
Personal loyalty always must give way
To patriotic duty.
                              Solidarity, friends,
Is what we need. The whole crew must close ranks.
The safety of our state depends upon it.
Our trust. Our friendships. Our security.
Good order in the city. And our greatness.

Understand therefore that I intend
To make good what I say by what I do.
And hear this first. This ordinance is binding.

Concerning the sons of Oedipus:
Eteocles, who fell in our defence,
Eteocles will be buried with full honours
As a hero of his country.
                              But his brother
Polyneices, an exile who came back
To visit us with fire and sword, a traitor,
An anti-Theban Theban prepared to kill

His countrymen in war, and desecrate
The shrines of his country's gods, hear this
About Polyneices:
                    He is forbidden
Any ceremonial whatsoever.
No keening, no interment, no observance
Of any of the rites. Hereby he is adjudged
A carcass for the dogs and birds to feed on.
And nobody, let it be understood,
Nobody is to treat him otherwise
Than as the obscenity he was and is.

This is where I stand when it comes to Thebes:
Never to grant traitors and subversives
Equal footing with loyal citizens,
But to honour patriots in life and death.

Chorus

Loud and clear, King Creon,
You have laid down the law.
You exercise the power.
Your regulations hold
For the living and dead.

Creon

And that is why I regard you from now on
As agents of the law.

Chorus

                    Younger men
Would be better for that job.

Creon

                    I don't mean
You should do work on the ground. Naturally
I have guards out there already as we speak.

Chorus

Then why do you call us 'agents of the law'?

Creon

I mean you're not to lend the least support
To anyone who'd go against the order.

Chorus

But who'd do that?
Who would choose to be dead?

Creon

Death, yes, it would be. But you never know.
There's always money lurking and I never
Underestimate the lure of money.

Enter Guard.

Guard

Sir, I wouldn't exactly say I was panting to get here.
Far from it. As a matter of fact, I was more for
turning back. I was over a barrel. One part of me was
saying, 'Only a loony would walk himself into this,'
and another part was saying, 'You'd be a bigger loony
not to get to Creon first.' It was, 'You take the high
road, I'll take the low road,' then, 'What's your
hurry?', then, 'Get a move on.' But when all was said
and done there was only one thing for it: get here, get
it out and get it over, no matter what. So here I am,
the old dog for the hard road. What will be, says I,
will be.

Creon

What has got you into this state, guard?

Guard

First off, boss, you must know I'm in the clear. I didn't
do the thing, I didn't see who did it and so, in fairness,
I shouldn't be blamed for it.

Creon

Why do you need such fences and defences?
Your news is hardly all that desperate.

Guard

Desperate enough to panic me, your honour.

Creon

Then get it out, man, as you say yourself,
And get it over.

Guard

Well, here's what it is. The corpse. Somebody has as
good as buried it. Somebody's after attending to it
right. Casting the earth on it and all the rest.

Creon

What are you saying? What man would dare do this?

Guard

That, for the life of me, I cannot tell. There wasn't so
much as a scrape left on the ground. No sign of pick-
work or that class of thing. No rut-marks from a
wheel. Nothing but the land, the old hard scrabble.
Whoever did it was a mystery man entirely. When the
sentry showed us this morning, we were stunned. The
corpse had actually gone and disappeared. But then it
turned out it was only hidden, under this coat of dust.
As if somebody had treated it, you know, just to be
on the safe side. Somebody observing all the customs.

There were no tears in the flesh, so it couldn't have
been wild animals or the dogs.

And then the row broke out, everybody shouting, one
man blaming the next and ready to fight to prove his
innocence. We'd have put our hands in fire to clear
ourselves. Swearing by this and that that we'd neither
done the deed nor knew who did it. And then, when
we'd more or less calmed down, one man speaks up
and panics us again And what he stated was the
obvious: you would have to be told, the thing could
be hid no longer. So that was agreed and I was the
lucky man. I drew the short straw and that, sir, 's why
I'm here. The one that's never welcome, the bearer of
bad news.

Chorus

Creon, sir, I cannot help but think
The gods have had a hand in this somewhere.

Creon

Enough. Don't anger me. Your age, my friend,
Still doesn't give you rights to talk such garbage.
The gods, you think, are going to attend
To this particular corpse? Preposterous.
Did they hide him under clay for his religion?
For coming to burn their colonnaded temples?
For attacking a city under their protection?
The gods, you think, will side with the likes of him?
Here's something else for you to think about.
For a good while now I have had reports
Of disaffected elements at work here,
A certain poisonous minority
Unready to admit the rule of law

And my law in particular.
                                I know
These people and how they operate.
                        Maybe they are not
The actual perpetrators, but they possess
The money and the means to bribe their way.
Money has a long and sinister reach.
It slips into the system, changes hands
And starts to eat away at the foundations
Of everything we stand for.
                            Money brings down leaders,
Warps minds, and generally corrupts
People and institutions. But in this case
Whoever took the bribe will pay the price.
                            You then: listen to this
For this is my solemn vow: if you do not
Apprehend, arrest and bring before me
The one who interred the corpse, I'll hang you out
And have you so carved up and pulled apart
You'll be pleading to be dead. You'll discover then
What interest your kind of money earns.
You can't, friend, have your palm greased and expect
To get away clean. Everything comes out.

Guard

Can I say a word or am I just dismissed?

Creon

Dismissed. That's it. You and your news disturb me.

Guard

Your conscience is what's doing the disturbing.

Creon

Watch it, guard. You're overstepping here.

Guard

It's that mystery man who has you really bothered.

Creon

I warn you. You had better mind your mouth.

Guard

But I didn't do it.

Creon

Oh yes, you did. The minute you smelt money.

Guard

What's happening here, Creon, is that the judge
Has misjudged everything.

Creon

And what I'm telling you
Is this: unless you expose the guilty party to me,
You'll rue the day you bought into this plot.

Exit Creon.

Guard

O yes, of course, expose him! Bring him in.
But be that as may be, this much is sure:
Yours truly won't be back here in a hurry.

Me that was done for!

Ye gods! Ye gods!

I'm off!

Exit Guard.

Chorus

Among the many wonders of the world
Where is the equal of this creature, man?
First he was shivering on the shore in skins,

Or hunched in a dug-out, terrified of drowning.
Then he took up oars, put tackle on a mast
And steered himself by the stars through gales.

Once upon a time from the womb of earth
The gods were born and he bowed down
To worship them. He worked the land,
Stubbed the forests and harnessed stallions.
His furrows cropped, he feasted his eyes
On hay and herds as far as the horizon.

The wind is no more swift or mysterious
Than his mind and words; he has mastered thinking,
Roofed his house against hail and rain
And worked out laws for living together.

Home-maker, thought-taker, measure of all things,
He can heal with herbs and read the heavens.
Nothing seems beyond him. When he yields to his gods,
When truth is the treadle of his loom
And justice the shuttle, he'll be shown respect –
The city will reward him. But let him once

Overstep what the city allows,
Tramp down right or treat the law
Wilfully, as his own word,
Then let this wonder of the world remember:
He'll have put himself beyond the pale.
When he comes begging we will turn our backs.

Enter Guard, leading Antigone.

Now what has happened? Is this
The gods at work?
Antigone, child of doom,
Have you gone and broken the law?

Guard

This is the one. We caught her at it,
Attending to the corpse. Where's Creon gone?

Chorus

Creon knows when he's needed. He's coming now.

Enter Creon.

Creon

Needed? Why am I needed?

Guard

King Creon. Sir.
There's no such thing as an oath that can't be broken.
Circumstances change and your mind changes.
After the going-over you gave me here
I swore I was off for good. But every now and then
The thing you'd hardly let yourself imagine
Actually happens. So here I am again.
And here's the one that was covering up the corpse.
I was on to her in a flash: my prisoner
And mine alone. No need to draw lots this time,
I can tell you.
And now, sir, she is yours.
It's up to you to judge her and convict her –
And let me go. I deserve to be discharged.
My job is done.

Creon

How did you come on her?

Guard

At her work, for all to see, interring Polyneices.

Creon

And you stand over this? This is the truth?

Guard

I saw her burying the body you said
Nobody was to bury. Will that do?

Creon

How was she observed and caught? Describe it.

Guard

Oh, I'll describe it. Gladly. After your tongue-lashing
I went back and joined the watch, and told them
We were all marked men. So we did what we could do.
We approached the corpse again and cleaned it down
And peeled away the clothes. It was going off
So we stationed ourselves at points around the hill –
Out of the wind, you know, because of the smell.
Every man on guard, watching the other man,
Ready to pounce the minute he nodded off –
And all the while there's this fireball of a sun
Going up and up the sky until at midday
You could hardly bear it. The ground was like a
                                         gridiron..

And then what happens? A whirlwind. Out of nowhere.
Leaves whipped off trees. Flying sand and dust.
The plain below us disappeared, and the path up,
And the hills on the horizon – like the sky was
Vomiting black air. So we closed our eyes
And braced ourselves for whatever plague it was
The gods were sending.
                            But then it clears
And this one's standing, crying her eyes out.
She sees the bare corpse and lets out a screech
And starts to curse whoever did the deed.
She was like a wild bird round an empty nest.

She lifted dust in her hands and let it fall.
She poured the water three times from her urn,
Taking care to do the whole thing right,
And showed no signs of panic when we trapped her,
Denied no thing she was accused of doing
Then or earlier.
                    But here's what's strange:
I felt a sadness coming over me.
It's one thing to be let off the hook yourself,
Another thing to land your friends in trouble.
But if I don't watch out for myself, who will?

Creon
    You there, studying the ground: hold up your head
    And tell us: is this true?

Antigone
                    True. I admit it.

Creon (*to Guard*)
    All right. You're in the clear – so now clear off.

    Exit Guard.

                    You then. Tell me
    And be quick about it: did you or did you not
    Know that the proclamation forbade all this?

Antigone
    I did know. How could I not? Didn't everybody?

Creon
    And still you dared to disobey the law?

Antigone
    I disobeyed because the law was not
    The law of Zeus nor the law ordained

20

By Justice, Justice dwelling deep
Among the gods of the dead. What they decree
Is immemorial and binding for us all.
The proclamation had your force behind it
But it was mortal force, and I, also a mortal,
I chose to disregard it. I abide
By statutes utter and immutable –
Unwritten, original, god-given laws.

Was I going to humour you, or honour gods?
Sooner or later I'll die anyhow
And sooner may be better in my case:
This death penalty is almost a relief.
If I had to live and suffer in the knowledge
That Polyneices was lying above ground
Insulted and defiled, that would be worse
Than having to suffer any doom of yours.
You think I'm just a reckless woman, but –
Never, Creon, forget:
You yourself could be the reckless one.

Chorus

This wildness in her comes from Oedipus.
She gets it from her father. She won't relent.

Creon

We'll wait and see. The bigger the resistance
The bigger the collapse.

                Iron that's forged the hardest
Snaps the quickest. Wild she may well be
But even the wildest horses come to heel
When they're reined and bitted right.

                Subordinates
Are just not made for insubordination.

When she defied the general order
Antigone had already gone too far,
But flaunting that defiance in my face
Puts her beyond the pale. Who does she think
She is? The man in charge?
                    Have I to be
The woman of the house and take her orders?
She has brought death sentences upon herself
And on her sister –
                    Yes, yes, yes,
Ismene is involved in this thing too.
The pair of them, my own sister's daughters,
In it, up to the hilt. But neither seed nor breed
Will save them now.
                    Get Ismene out here.
She was inside in the house a while ago,
Raving, out of her mind.
                    That's how guilt
Affects some people. They simply break
And everything comes out.
                    But the barefaced ones,
The ones who defy you when they're found out,
They're worse again.

Antigone
                    Will it be enough for you
To see me executed?

Creon
                    More than enough.

Antigone
Then why don't you do it quickly?
Anything I have to say to you

Or you to me is sheer exacerbation.
I never did a nobler thing than bury
My brother Polyneices. And if these men
Weren't so afraid to sound unpatriotic
They'd say the same. But you are king
And because you're king you won't be contradicted.

Creon

So you know something no one else in Thebes knows?

Antigone

They know it too. They're just afraid to say it.

Creon

But you're so high and mighty you've no qualms.

Antigone

None. There's no shame in burying a brother.

Creon

Your brother Eteocles also died in the war.

Antigone

My father's and my mother's son, yes, dead.

Creon

– And dishonoured, when you honour Polyneices.

Antigone

The dead aren't going to begrudge the dead.

Creon

So wrongdoers and the ones wronged fare the same?

Antigone

Polyneices was no common criminal.

Creon

He terrorised us. Eteocles stood by us.

Antigone

Religion dictates the burial of the dead.

Creon

Dictates the same for loyal and disloyal?

Antigone

Who knows what loyalty is in the underworld?

Creon

Even there, I'd know my enemy.

Antigone

And I would know my friend. Where I assist
With love, you set at odds.

Creon

Go then and love your fill in the underworld.
No woman will dictate the law to me.

Ismene is brought in.

Chorus

Ismene, look, in tears!
For her sister. For herself.

Creon

You bloodsucker. You two-faced parasite.
The pair of you at me like a pair of leeches!
Two vipers spitting venom at the throne.
Speak, you, now. You helped her, didn't you?
Or are you going to claim you're innocent?

Ismene

I helped her, yes, if I'm allowed to say so
And now I stand with her to take what comes.

Antigone

I don't allow this. Justice won't allow it.
You wouldn't help.
                    We cut all ties.
                                It's over.

Ismene

But now I'm with you. I want to throw myself
Like a lifeline to you in your sea of troubles.

Antigone

Too late, my sister. You chose a safe line first.
The dead and Hades know who did this deed.

Ismene

Antigone, don't rob me of all honour.
Let me die with you and act right by the dead.

Antigone

You can't just pluck your honour off a bush
You didn't plant. You forfeited your right.

Ismene

If Antigone dies, how will I keep on living?

Antigone

Ask Creon, since you seem so fond of him.

Ismene

What good does it do you, twisting the knife like this?

Antigone

I can't help it, dear heart. It hurts me too.

Ismene

But even at this stage, can I not do something?

Antigone

You can save yourself. That is my honest wish.

Ismene

And be for ever shamed in my own eyes?

Antigone

You made a choice, you bear the consequence.

Ismene

I was against your choice and made it clear.

Antigone

One world stood by you, one stood by me.

Ismene

Different worlds, both equally offended.

Antigone

Take heart, Ismene: you are still alive
But I have long gone over to the dead.

Creon

This is incredible: one of these
Had the father's madness in her from the start
But I never thought to see it in Ismene.

Ismene

You think, Creon, when you drive us to the edge
We won't go over?

Creon

You went over long ago,
The minute you linked up with this one here.

Ismene

My sister is the mainstay of my life.

Creon

Your sister was . . . There's no 'is' any more.

Ismene

You mean you'd kill your own son's bride-to-be?

Creon

I would and will. He has other fields to plough.

Ismene

He loves her utterly. For him, there's no one else.

Creon

No son of mine will take a condemned wife.

Ismene

O poor, poor Haemon! To have you for a father!

Creon

You and your marriage talk. Too late for that.

Chorus

Do you mean, sir, you'll rob Haemon of this woman?

Creon

Hades will rob him first.

Chorus

                        The sentence, though,
Has been decided on?

Creon

               It has, by me,
And I, remember, have your acclamation.
Get her away from here. And the other one.
Women were never meant for this assembly.
From now on they'll be kept in place again
And better be . . .
                  Yes, keep an eye on them.
Once the end's in sight they all get desperate.
Even the bravest will make a run for it.

27

Antigone and Ismene are led out.

Chorus
Whoever has been spared the worst is lucky.
When high gods shake a house
That family is going to feel the blow
Generation after generation.
It starts like an undulation underwater,
A surge that hauls black sand up off the bottom,
Then turns itself into a tidal current
Lashing the shingle and shaking promontories.

I see the sorrows of this ancient house
Break on the inmates and keep breaking on them
Like foaming wave on wave across a strand.
They stagger to their feet and struggle on
But the gods do not relent, the living fall
Where the dead fell in their day
Generation after generation.

And now a light that seemed about to glow,
A hope for the house of Oedipus, has died.
Dust cast upon a corpse extinguished it.
Bloodstained dust. A defiant spirit.
The fury and backlash of overbearing words.

O Zeus on high, beyond all human reach,
Nothing outwits you and nothing ever will.
You cannot be lulled by sleep or slowed by time.
O dazzle on Olympus, O power made light,
Now and forever your law is manifest:
No windfall or good fortune comes to mortals
That isn't paid for in the coin of pain.

Here is what happens: hope and mad ambition
Are many a time fulfilled for many a man;
But just as often they are will-o'-the-wisps
That'll send him wild-eyed into fire and flood.
Well has it been said: the man obsessed
Is a cock-of-the-walk in a hurry towards the worst.
Our luck is little more than a short reprieve
That the gods allow.

But look, there's Haemon.

Be easy with him, sir.
Allow a youngest son to say his say.
He'll be beyond himself. He'll have gone wild.
He'll know his father doomed his bride to death.

Enter Haemon.

Creon

Unlike you gentlemen, I don't possess
Clairvoyant powers. I prefer to wait
And hear what Haemon has to say himself.

Haemon, son, the judgement I pronounced
Is what the law requires. Are you coming here
To rant and rage against me, or are we still
Father dear and father's son, as ever?

Haemon

Yes, father. Father's son . . . I do rely
On your wisdom and experience and would want
No match or marriage to displace you ever.

Creon

That's how it is and how it should be, Haemon.
It's right for the son to heed his father's judgement.

It's what all men pray for,
Children who will show a due respect,
Who will make their father's enemies
Their enemies, and his friends their friends.
Nothing gives an enemy more pleasure
Than to see you let down by the child you've reared:
That is a bitter pill to have to swallow.
Don't, Haemon, lose your wits over a woman.
You're wild for her, but once the thing is done
There and then she'll turn cold comfort.
Nothing's worse than marrying yourself
To a woman that's no good. Nothing cuts as deep
As when the one who's closest turns against you.
That's why I say: have nothing to do with her.
If she needs a husband, let Hades find her one,
For of this you can be certain: I won't be making
A liar of myself in front of the city.
She, and she alone, defied the order
Openly and deliberately, so she shall perish.

Let her beseech Zeus to her heart's content
To guarantee the bond of family blood:
My family too have bonds they need to honour.
They must observe the discipline I expect
From every citizen. The city has to see
The standards of a public man reflected
In his private conduct. He has to be a man
Ready to abide by his own orders,
A comrade you'd depend on in a battle.
When discipline goes, self-discipline goes as well
And once that happens cities, homes and armies
Collapse, inevitably. Failure of rule
Is the most destructive thing. Obedience

And respect must be instilled. And that is why
No woman here is going to be allowed
To walk all over us. Otherwise, as men
We'll be disgraced. We won't deserve the name.

Chorus

Well, we are old men, so perhaps our judgement's shaky,
But what you're saying seems to make good sense.

Haemon

The use of reason, father . . . The gods
Have given us the use of reason.
But do we use it right? Do I? Do you?
It's hard to know, but this much I can tell you:
When you hear things you'd rather not be hearing
You get worked up. So therefore people shield you.
But not me, father. I hear everything
Or overhear it. And all that's talked about
In this city now is Antigone.
People are heartbroken for her. What,
They're asking, did she do so wrong? What deserves
A punishment like this? As far as they're concerned,
She should be honoured – a woman who rebelled!
Rebelled when her brother's corpse was being thrown
To the carrion crows. *She was heroic!*
That's what's being said behind closed doors.

Believe me, father, nothing means more to me
Than you and your good name. What else could?
Father/son, son/father – that regard
Is natural and mutual.

For your own sake, then,
I ask you: reconsider. Nobody,
Nobody can be sure they're always right.

The ones who are fullest of themselves that way
Are the emptiest vessels. There's no shame
In taking good advice.
                              It's a sign of wisdom.
                              If a river floods
The trees on the bank that bend to it survive.
If a skipper doesn't slacken sail in storm
His whole crew ends up clinging to the keel.
So. Swallow pride and anger. Allow yourself
To change.

I'm young, I know, but I offer you this thought:
All of us would like to have been born
Infallible, but since we know we weren't,
It's better to attend to those who speak
In honesty and good faith, and learn from them.

Chorus

You should take good note, Creon, of Haemon's words
And he of yours. Both of you say sound things.

Creon

So a man of my age, you are telling me,
Must take instruction from a man of his?

Haemon

Only if it is the right instruction.
The rightness is what matters, not the age.

Creon

Rightness? What rightness? Aren't you against the law?

Haemon

I am not, and I don't want you to be.

Creon

But isn't that why Antigone's a danger?

Haemon

People here in Thebes don't seem to think so.

Creon

Do my orders come from Thebes and from the people?

Haemon

Can you hear yourself? What age do you sound now?

Creon

Who's to take charge? The ruler or the ruled?

Haemon

There's no city that belongs in single hands.

Creon

Rulers, I thought, were meant to be in charge.

Haemon

Where you should be in charge is in a desert.

Creon

Listen to him. He's on the woman's side.

Haemon

Are you a woman? I'm on your side, father.

Creon

On my side, but always going against me?

Haemon

Not against *you*. Against your going wrong.

Creon

Am I wrong to wield the powers vested in me?

Haemon
Do they give you rights to disregard the gods?

Creon
Son, you're pathetic. You give in to a woman.

Haemon
But to nothing that's forbidden or wrong.

Creon
Everything you say is on her behalf.

Haemon
And yours and mine and the gods' under the earth.

Creon
You'll never marry her while she draws breath.

Haemon
Then she'll have to die, and she won't die on her own.

Creon
Has it come to this? Is this an open threat?

Haemon
It's my resolution. Read it as you wish.

Creon
You'll rue the day you took it on yourself
To lecture me. You're a real know-nothing.

Haemon
If you weren't my father, father –

Creon
                          That's enough.
The woman has you round her little finger.

Haemon

Shutting me up still doesn't make you right.

Creon

By all the gods that look down from Olympus,
I'm telling you you'll pay a heavy price
For this disrespect.
                    Bring her out here.
Bring her out and do away with her
So that her groom can watch the deed being done.

Haemon

Never. And never, father, again
Will you set eyes on me. You're deranged.
Let whoever can abide you watch her die.

Exit Haemon.

Chorus

King Creon – a younger man like that,
Out of control – he could do anything.

Creon

He can do his worst then, and good luck to him.
It won't affect the fate of those two women.

Chorus

Two, you say? Have you condemned them both?

Creon

No, you are right. One didn't lift a finger.

Chorus

But Antigone. You've actually considered
How you're going to put Antigone to death?

Creon

    Up in the rocks, up where nobody goes,
    There's a steep path that leads higher, to a cave.
    She'll be put in there and some food put in with her –
    To ward off any blood-guilt from the city.
    And once she's in, she can pray to her heart's content
    To her god of death. After all her Hades talk,
    It'll be her chance to see if he can save her.

    Exit Creon.

Chorus

    Love that can't be withstood,
    Love that scatters fortunes,
    Love like a green fern shading
    The cheek of a sleeping girl.
    Love like spume off a wave
    Or turf-smoke in the air,
    Love, you wield your power
    Over mortal and immortal
    And you put them mad.

    Love leads the good astray,
    Plays havoc in heart and home;
    You, love, here and now
    In this tormented house
    Are letting madness loose.
    The unabashed gaze of a bride
    Breeds desire and danger.
    Eternal, sexual, smiling,
    The goddess Aphrodite
    Is irresistible.
    Love mounts to the throne with law.

    Antigone is led in under guard.

But the law and all it stands for
Cannot hold back my tears.
Antigone, you are a bride,
Being given away to death.

Antigone
Given away to death!
Remember this, citizens.
I am linked on Hades' arm,
Taking my last look,
My last walk in the light.
Soon the sun will go out
On a silent, starless shore
And Hades will step aside.
He will give me to Acheron,
Lord of the pitch-black lake,
And that bridegroom's cold hand
Will take my hand in the dark.

Chorus
Steadfast Antigone,
Never before did Death
Open his stone door
To one so radiant.
You would not live a lie.
Vindicated, lauded,
Age and disease outwitted,
You go with head held high.

Antigone
I am like Niobe,
Niobe turned to stone
In the thawing snow and rain,
A rock that weeps forever

Like ivy in a shower
Sluicing down the ridge
Of high Mount Sipylus.

Chorus

Niobe was immortal,
Sky-born, far beyond us,
For we are born of the earth.
But someone as glorious
In life and in death as you
Can also seem immortal.

Antigone

Stop. Enough. Don't mock.
Wait, at least, till I'm gone.
I am still in life, and I dread
To leave our groves and springs.
O fortunate men of Thebes,
O my Thebes of the chariots,
Farewell. I am going away
Under my rock-piled roof.
No mourner waits at the mound.
I'll be shut in my halfway house,
Unwept by those alive,
Unwelcomed as yet by the dead.

Chorus

Ah, child, you were carried away
But now you're halted and hauled
Before implacable Justice,
Paying, perhaps, in your life
For the past life of your father.

Antigone

There. You have hit home.

Over and over again
Because I am who I am
I retrace that fatal line
And the ghastly love I sprang from.
My father weds his mother.
He mounts her. Me and mine,
His half-sisters and brothers,
Are born in their sullied bed.
These are the stricken dead
I go to meet in Hades.

Chorus

You go because you were noble.
Nobility mitigates
The offence you gave; but power
And everyone who wields it
Will brook no opposition.
You were headstrong and self-willed
And now you suffer for it.

Antigone

No flinching then at fate.
No wedding guests. No wake.
No keen. No panegyric.
I close my eye on the sun.
I turn my back on the light.

Enter Creon.

Creon

If people had the chance to keen themselves
Before they died, they'd weep and wail forever:
That's enough.

         Just get her ready and march.
March to the rock vault, wall her in and leave.

After that it'll be up to her to choose.
She can live there under dry stone, or can die.
There's no blood on my hands here. It was she
Who put herself beyond the pale. She is to blame
For every blackout stone they pile up round her.

Antigone
Stone of my wedding chamber, stone of my tomb,
Stone of my prison roof and prison floor,
Behind you and beyond you stand the dead.
They are my people and they're waiting for me
And when they see me coming down the road
They'll hurry out to meet me, all of them.
My father and my mother first, and then
Eteocles, my brother – every one
As dear to me as when I washed and dressed
And laid them out.
                        But Polyneices,
When I did the same for you, when I did
What people know in their hearts of hearts
Was right, I was doomed for it.

Not for a husband, not even for a son
Would I have broken the law.
Another husband I could always find
And have other sons by him if one were lost.
But with my father gone, and my mother gone,
Where can I find another brother, ever?
The law of this same logic I obeyed
When I disobeyed Creon. It's a rule of life,
But all Creon can see is a crazy girl
He must get rid of.
                        Have I offended gods?
Do the gods have no regard for what I did?

Where can I turn if they have turned away?
The right observance put me in the wrong:
And if that is the gods' verdict, so be it.
I'll have transgressed and will suffer gladly.
But if the wrong was laid upon me wrongly
By these unjust ones, then let their penalty
Be no less than the one they've doomed me to.

Chorus

She's still unreconciled, as driven as ever.

Creon

The quicker then they move her on, the better.

Antigone

This man's words are as cold as death itself.

Creon

They're meant to be. Meant to destroy your hope.
The sentence stands. The law will take its course.

Antigone

Now gods of Thebes, look down.
Through my native streets and fields
I'm being marched away.
And never, you men of Thebes,
Forget what you saw today:
Oedipus's daughter,
The last of his royal house
Condemned. And condemned for what?
For practising devotion,
For a reverence that was right.

Antigone is led out.

Chorus

Danae too was walled up in the dark,
Princess daughter imprisoned by her father,
Barred and bolted in a tower of brass.

Then molten Zeus, a battering ray of light
(O flash and cloudburst, blossom-stripping shower)
Ungirdled and dishevelled her with gold.

Fate finds strange ways to fulfil its ends.
Not military power nor the power of money,
Not battlements of stone nor black-hulled fleets

Can fend off fate or keep its force at bay.
Blood under maenads' nails, on the mountain path,
Cries on the wind, weeping heard in the palace.

Whoever has been spared the worst is lucky.

Enter Tiresias, blind, led by a boy.

Tiresias

My lord, my countrymen, I know you're there.
We have been going the roads, the pair of us
Going by the one same pair of eyes.
The man that's blinded always needs a guide.

Creon

Tiresias, you venerable man:
What news have you brought for me this time?

Tiresias

News that you would be as well to heed.

Creon

When did I not, prophetic father, heed you?

Tiresias

And isn't that why your ship has stayed on course?

Creon

You kept me right. I know it. In my bones.

Tiresias

Then know this: where you are standing now
Is a cliff edge, and there's cold wind blowing.

Creon

Why do you always put that shiver through me?

Tiresias

Because I have the power to see and warn.
I know things once I sit in that stone chair
And the birds begin to skirl above my head.
But never in all my years have I heard the likes
Of the screams and screeches that I heard this day.
There was no meaning to them. I knew by the whirl
of wings
And the rips and spits of blood the birds were mad.

I was afraid, so once the blaze was lit
On the altar stone I brought my offerings,
But the fire had no effect. It wouldn't take
And none of the bits would burn.
Slime,
Slime was what I got instead of flame.
Matter oozing out from near the bone.
The fat stayed raw and wept into the ash.
Everywhere there was this spattered gall
From the burst gall-bladder. Slurry, smoke and dirt . . .
Some deep fault caused that. The boy here saw it
And I rely on him as much as you

On me . . .
                    There was no sign to be read.
                                        The rite had failed.

Because of you, Creon. You and your headstrongness.

That body lying out there decomposing
Is where the contagion starts. The dogs and birds
Are at it day and night, spreading reek and rot
On every altar stone and temple step, and the gods
Are revolted. That's why we have this plague,
This vile pollution. That's why my birds in flight
Aren't making sense. They're feeding on his flesh.

Consider well, my son. All men make mistakes.
But mistakes don't have to be forever,
They can be admitted and atoned for.
It's the overbearing man who is to blame.
Pull back. Yield to the dead. Don't stab a ghost.
What can you win when you only wound a corpse?
I have your good at heart, and have good advice.
The easiest thing for you would be to take it.

Creon
Why am I standing out here like a target?
Why is every arrow aimed at me?
                                You, Tiresias,
You and your whole fortune-telling tribe
Have bled me white. But not any more.
Whoever wants can cross your palm with silver
But they still won't get that body under ground.
None of your pollution talk scares me.
Not if Zeus himself were to send his eagle
To scavenge on that flesh and shit it down,
Not even that would put me back on my word.

Nothing done on earth can defile the gods.
But even the wisest man on earth, old man,
Has been corrupted the minute he's prepared
To deliver fake truths on demand, for bribes.

Tiresias
This is bad. Does nobody realise –

Creon
Does nobody realise what?

Tiresias
Honest advice is not a thing you buy.

Creon
And witlessness has to be the greatest threat.

Tiresias
As you should know. It is your problem, Creon.

Creon
I don't want to trade insults with a prophet.

Tiresias
It's an insult to imply I am a fake.

Creon
All of you so-called seers: you have your price.

Tiresias
Rulers too have a name for being corrupt.

Creon
You realise you are talking to your king?

Tiresias
A king my words once helped to save this city.

Creon
Your second sight has been well warped since then.

Tiresias

My second sight scares me and should scare you.

Creon

Scare me then, but don't expect a bribe.

Tiresias

Talk of bribes won't shield you from the truth.

Creon

The decisions that I take aren't up for sale.

Tiresias

Then listen, Creon, and listen carefully.
The sun won't ride his chariot round the sky
Very much longer before flesh of your flesh
Answers corpse for corpse for your enactments.
This is what you'll get for thrusting down
A daughter of the sunlight to the shades.
You have buried her alive, and among the living
You have forbidden burial of one dead,
One who belongs by right to the gods below.
You have violated their prerogatives.
No earthly power, no god in upper air
Exerts authority over the dead.
Henceforth, therefore, there lie in wait for you
The inexorable ones, the Furies who destroy.
Then tell me, when the lamentation starts,
When woman-wail and man-howl rake your walls,
Tell me I've been bribed. And tell me it again
When enemy cities rise to avenge each corpse
You left dishonoured on the battlefield.
They turned to filth, remember, and the crows
Puddled and poked in it and would fly back
To foul each city with droppings of its dead.

I am not the target. I am the archer.
My shafts are tipped with truth and they stick deep.
Come, boy, take me home. Let him affront
Somebody younger now, and learn to control
His tongue, and see things in truer light.

Exit Tiresias and boy.

Chorus

He's gone, my lord, but his words won't go away.
Never, in all my days, was that man wrong.
When he warned the city, the city knew to listen.

Creon

I know. I listened too. And learned from him.
I hate a climb-down, but something's gathering head.

Chorus

Now, of all times, you must heed good advice.

Creon

What's to be done? Tell me and I'll do it.

Chorus

Set the girl free from behind the rocks
And make a burial mound for her brother's corpse.

Creon

You want me to renege?

Chorus

Immediately, in case the gods strike first.

Creon

It goes against the grain. But I am beaten.
Fate has the upper hand.

Chorus

Do it then, and do it yourself, quickly.

Creon

Right.

All hands get a move on, here and now.
The judgement is reversed. Take your crowbars,
Take picks up to the hill. I walled her in
And therefore I'll be there to bring her out.
In my heart of hearts I know what must be done.
Until we breathe our last breath we should keep
The established law.

Exit Creon with attendants.

Chorus

Call up the god of Thebes,
Son of thundering Zeus,
Fleet foot and open hand.

We who live where Cadmus
Sowed the dragon's teeth
Call on you, Dionysus –

Vine-man, pine-god, prince
Of the ivy bunch and wine cup,
We glory in your names.

From Delphi's high-faced cliff,
From the sunk Castalian spring,
From hillsides of ripe grapes

Come brilliantly to Thebes,
Thebes where the bright bolt struck
And begot you on Semele.

Now plague has struck your birthplace.
O Dionysus, appear
With men and maenads headlong

And dance the world to rights.
Be sunlight from Parnassus
Adazzle on the gulf,

Be the necklace-fire of stars,
The cauterising lightning.
Bewilder us with good.

We who live where Cadmus
Sowed the dragon's teeth
Call on you, Dionysus.

Enter Messenger.

Messenger
Old neighbours, elder citizens, you don't need me
To tell you about life. You've seen it all.
Nobody can predict what lies ahead.
Take our own man, Creon. Creon saved us,
Saved the country, and there he was, strong king,
Strong head of family, the man in charge.
And now it's all been lost. He might as well
Be dead, for when you lose your happiness,
I always say, you lose your life.
                       You can dwell in state,
Have all the trappings of success and style,
But if you can't enjoy them in your heart,
What does it mean? If your joy in life's destroyed,
You're left with a mirage. Shadows and ash.

Chorus
Is this more bad news for the royal house?

Messenger
Dead. They are dead. And the living bear the guilt.

Chorus
Who was killed? Who did the killing? Quick!

Messenger
Haemon was killed –

Chorus
                    But by himself or Creon?

Messenger
By himself. For the blood on his father's hands.

Chorus
Tiresias, mighty seer, it has come to pass!

Messenger
We must make sense of it as best we can.

Chorus
Eurydice!
            The queen, look, 's on her way.
Distracted. She must have heard the news.

Enter Eurydice.

Eurydice
I am in dread. My hand was on the latch
Of the little gate into the temple shrine . . .
Then I heard keening in the house, and fainted.
O citizens, there's not anybody here
Knows better than I what wailing like that means.
I know what to expect. Just say what happened.

Messenger
I can tell you the whole thing, ma'am. There's no sense
In making a liar of myself.
Right from the start I was at your husband's side,

All of us climbing the hill. And sure enough
It was still there, Polyneices' corpse,
Or what the dogs had left of it. So we prayed
To the goddess of the crossroads and to Pluto
To hold their anger back and to ignore
The pitilessness of that desecration.
Then we washed the remains in purifying water,
Gathered sticks and made enough of a fire
To burn him decently. And as was right,
We piled his home ground over him at last.

Then on we went, right up to the cave mouth,
And deep in that unholy vault we hear
Such terrible howling we have to send for Creon.
And when Creon comes, he howls himself and he

knows.

'O hide me, hide me from myself,' he cries,
'For I face the saddest door I ever faced.
I hear my son's voice in there. Come on,'
He shouts, 'Tumble the stones, break through
And look and tell me. Tell me if it's Haemon.'

So we broke the barrier down as ordered
And saw into the gallery. Antigone was there,
Hanging by her neck from a linen noose,
And Haemon on the ground beside her
With his arms up round her waist, imploring
The underworld, lamenting his dead bride
And shouting execrations against Creon.

But Creon couldn't help himself and went
With open arms to the boy and started pleading,
Calling him 'son', saying he'd had a fit
And to watch himself. But Haemon spat in his face

And made a quick lunge with his two-edged sword
And would have got him if Creon hadn't dodged.
Then before we knew where we were, he had turned
The sword on himself and buried half the blade
In his own side. And as he was collapsing
His arms still clung to the girl and blood came spurting
Out of his mouth all over her white cheek . . .
That was the kiss he gave his bride-to-be.

Eurydice begins her exit.

A wedding witnessed in the halls of death.

And one to teach us living witnesses
The mortal cost of ill-judged words and deeds.

Chorus
But not a word from her. I wish there'd been
A cry at least or a sigh or a single tear.

Messenger
                                    Maybe now
She needs her privacy inside the house.
Maybe she can't give vent to grief in public.
I hope that's it. I too am afraid.

Chorus
That silence is a danger in itself.

Messenger
She shouldn't be going in there unattended.

*Exit Messenger, and from the side enter Creon, with
Haemon's body.*

Chorus
Look. Stand back. It's the king
Coming to bury his own.

How did the likes of us
Foresee this and not him?

Creon

Make way for your king of wrong.
Wrong-headed on the throne,
Wrong-headed in the home,
Wrong-footed by the heavens.
And you, dear son, dead son,
I was wrong to harry you.

Chorus

Too late, alas, you've learned.

Creon

The hammer-blow of justice
Has caught me and brought me low.
I am under the wheels of the world.
Smashed to bits by a god.

Enter Messenger.

Messenger

My lord, you come bowed down with grief enough,
But you must brace yourself to suffer more.

Creon

What can be worse than worst?
What has happened now?

Messenger

The one who brought your son into the world
Has taken leave of it. Your queen's life-blood
Is on the palace floor.

Creon

Let the hounds of Hades lick it!

Why am I clamped like prey
In the hungry jaws of death?
I'm a kill that death has made
And attacked for the second time.
Your words are tooth and claw.
Say again the news of the queen.

The corpse of Eurydice is revealed.

Chorus
It doesn't need to be said.
It cannot be kept hidden.

Creon
Mother. And child. Both.
I have wived and fathered death.

Messenger
No, my lord. She dealt the stroke herself.
The sword was two-edged, and so was her grief
For her two sons, for Megareus killed
Defending Thebes and Haemon who killed himself.
But then as the dark stole down over her eyes,
She called you death-dealer and cursed your name.

Creon
Why doesn't somebody take
A two-edged sword to me?
The dark is on me too.
I'm at bay in guilt and grief.

Messenger
Death-dealer, she said, because you and your doings
Felled her children.

Creon

And then she raised her hand
To do the deed?

Messenger

When she'd listened to how Haemon stabbed himself
She went and took your own sword from its scabbard
And buried it in her heart.

Creon

Let every verdict be pronounced
Against me. She was guiltless.
It was my hand on the hilt,
My hand that drove the blade.
Take me out of your sight.
I am nothing now.
Forget me. Treat me as nothing.

Chorus

This is right, if right can ever come
From wrongs like yours. This is good.
When the worst has to be faced, the best thing is
To face it quickly.

Creon

The quicker it comes, the better.
I want to hurry death.
I want to be free of the dread
Of wakening in the morning.
Waking up at night.
All I pray for now
Is the dawn of my last day.

Chorus

Bear with the present; what will be will be.
The future is cloth waiting to be cut.

Creon

I still have prayed my prayer.

Chorus

You have prayed enough.
There is no protection.
You courted calamity.
Resign yourself.

Creon

Take me, hide me, blindfold me from these
And keep your distance. Everything I've touched
I have destroyed. I've nobody to turn to,
Nowhere I can go. My recklessness and pride
I paid for in the end. The blow came quick.

Exit Creon.

Chorus

Wise conduct is the key to happiness.
Always rule by the gods and reverence them.
Those who overbear will be brought to grief.
Fate will flail them on its winnowing floor
And in due season teach them to be wise.